Letters From My Broken Heart

Serena Lammi

Presentation by *BookLeaf Publishing*

Web: www.bookleafpub.com

E-mail: info@bookleafpub.com

ISBN: 9789358367331

First edition 2023

To the love of my life and best friend. Our love stands the test of time, even after all these years. You'll always have your place in the rooms of my heart.

Here We Are Again

Here we are again...

Together in a moment
I didn't think would ever again be.

Your smile, your laughter,
The way you're looking at me.

Time has stopped and the
World is melting away.

But these small moments are brief
And fleeting to my dismay.

Reality disappears and nothing
Else matters during our time.

Our souls are connected,
You will always be mine.

It's a forever kind of love bond
That we share.

We know that no matter what
It will always be there.

Nothing and no one can
Take this from us.

We are more than just
Physical driven by lust.

You've taken up root in
Every room in my heart.

I feel your presence even
When we are apart.

Here we are again...

I Haven't Forgotten

I haven't forgotten the shine in your eyes, when you would tell me I'm beautiful.

I haven't forgotten the sparks of electricity surging through our bodies when my skin would graze upon yours.

I haven't forgotten the butterflies in my stomach, the drop and the elevation, I felt when you would kiss my lips, pushing yours into mine.

I haven't forgotten the tingles from my head to my feet when you would make me quiver and twitch at the height of pleasure.

I haven't forgotten the love that filled my heart for you....

I haven't forgotten the crushing pain I felt in my soul, ripping my heart into pieces when you walked away.

I haven't forgotten the countless nights the tears would flow past midnight when I would mourn your loss.

I haven't forgotten the loneliness of the cold bed
void of emotion when you left.

I haven't forgotten the butterflies flitting turning
to knives twisting my insides when I thought of
you.

I haven't forgotten the anger and rage as red as
blood and hot as lava that would course through
my veins, burning you out of me.

I haven't forgotten how broken I felt when you
stopped loving me.

Does My Love

5

Does my love reach you over distance and time?
Does my love still make your eyes smile and
shine?
Does my love reach into the depths of your soul?
Does my love make you feel young, never
growing old?

Resurfaced

When I think about you,
My face smiles but my heart hurts.
Memories of us flood my present
With all the unresolved emotions at their side.
I thought I tucked you deep, deep away
In the rooms of my heart.
But you have resurfaced.
I see your fingertips upon my skin,
Your lips graze against mine.
I hear your heart whisper to my soul,
And I feel your voice stopping time.

9 years had passed and our lives grew apart.
But the moment I looked into your eyes
It all came flooding back.
Resurfaced all at once.

The love, the lust, the toxicity of us.
The rush and warmth of our bodies touch.
The acceptance and understanding
That connected us from the start.

Now that you have resurfaced,
How long will you stay up for air?

Only You

The ghost of you haunts the rooms of my heart.
There is no room for any other occupant.
Each door opens another piece of you.
Love, anger, joy, sadness, bliss and grief.
All of them dedicated to you.

You Do This To Me

I catch my breath
My heart skips a beat
The butterflies drop
I am elevated by your touch

My soul it smiles
Your voice surrounds me
Blanketing my skin
I am driven not just by lust

I hold more than love in this
Heart of mine for you
Kindness, joy and a little
Bit of anger too.

Fairytale

Once upon a time
Many moons ago
You looked into my eyes
Deep into my soul

Your eyes so blue
Your smile so bright
Your touch so warm
I melted at first sight

I was naive
I didn't have a clue
That one Night would
Become a lifetime with you

Like Romeo and Juliet
Crazy in love the both of us
Time passes by
And it becomes more than lust.

You're my Prince Charming
And I'm your Snow White
You have this darkness in you
But I am Your shining light

There is no riding off
Into the sunset
No this fairytale
Doesn't end like that

There is no happy ending
No songs to be sung
Just broken hearts
And airless lungs

Used

The scar tissue is fresh
And a constant reminder
Of when you held
My heart in your hands
And ripped it apart

The tears swelled in my eyes
I begged you not to do it
But you didn't listen
You dismissed my cries of agony
You took all the love
And left me the hate

I felt so used up and discarded
I served a purpose,
To appease your desires
When you were done
You threw me back where you found me

Hate You

I wish I could hate you
I wish I could forget you

I try
Oh boy do I try

I wish I never laid eyes on you
I wish I never felt your touch

I wish I wasn't so forgiving
I wish I could say no

I wish I could hate you....

But I Don't Even Care

When it comes to you...

No isn't in my vocabulary
I have no boundaries
I look like a desperate fool
But I don't even care

I'd do anything for you
You're bad for me
Nothing good will come of this
But I don't even care

There's a spark that ignites
Whenever we touch
It will burn the both of us
But I don't even care

I Wasn't Ready For Goodbye

I thought the worst pain I'd ever felt
Was when you walked away
When you no longer needed me

I wasn't ready for goodbye

I thought the wettest tears I'd ever cry
Were on those lonely nights that
Drenched my pillows and drowned my heart

I wasn't ready for goodbye

I thought the loneliness would subside but I
missed you more and more

I wasn't ready for goodbye

But now I know...

I'll always feel the pain
I'll always cry the tears
I'll always be lonely

Because I wasn't ready for goodbye

Hell Was Loving You

I feel my heart breaking
Tearing and crushing
Until there's a hole in my chest

There's a tightness in my breath
And I'm drowning
In memories of love and lust

I feel the fire burning in my soul
Something so deep and
I'd walk the depths of hell for you

Then I remembered hell was loving you.

It's an eternity of torture
Knowing you'll never be mine
Coveting the life that I wish I had

It's me putting my hand in the fire over and over
again
Expecting a different result

It's seeing you love someone else
More than me
And choosing that life over us

But you were never truly mine
And loving you will always be hell

Please

Please
Just rip my bleeding heart from my hands

Please
Just set my skin on fire with gasoline

Please
Just poke my eyes out with
An ice pick

Please
Just amputate my limbs with
A dull knife

But please
Please
Just don't tell me
You don't love me anymore

Intimacy

I have this idea of you and I...
We're the best of lovers and friends
You know how to light up a room
And you make me smile and laugh
You know how to love me right
And you make me swoon
It's not the sex
It's the intimacy
That sparks a fire between us two
The way your eyes smile at mine
Telling me I love you, Bee, always

Full of Love

My heart is overflowing
With such joy, passion and love.
My stomach is dropping
And elevating right into my head.

I'm weak, I'm dizzy, I lose my balance quite
often.

I'm full of love for you.
My soul is bound to yours.
More than lovers and friends,
We share a special connection.

It can't be duplicated and
Not everyone understands,
How we love each other
After all these years.

Your heart is full of love for me.

Bandages & Bruises

I'm all beat up
I have bruises on my heart

They're your fingerprints
From you squeezing it

Even though it hurt so much
I still don't want to be apart

The tears continue to flow
My soul is weeping.

Harder and harder until
I can no longer see

I have bandages wrapping me tight
I want to lie next to you sleeping

Why won't you stay with me tonight
I'll rub your head while you hold me

I love the way you kiss
I love the way you look my way

Even though I'm covered in bruises bandages
And the pain is not hard to see.

Forever

I could tell you forever
I could tell you right now
How much I love you
How much I care

I look into those blue eyes
And I just melt
I kiss those soft lips
And my knees go weak

I smell you on my skin
And my body quivers
I feel your sensual touch
And I know you're forever mine.

Time To Say Goodbye

What am I even doing with my life right now?

I ask myself this question, every time I walk
down the stairs to meet you.

I don't know why I put myself through this
heartache, because
Every time I look at you,
I know you will never be only mine.

I know it will never be us
Against the world.
I know it will never be me
You kiss goodnight or lie next to
While you're fast asleep in the night.
I know it will never be me.

As much as I don't want to...
As much as I feel I need you...
As much as I want to hold onto you and never
let go...

It's time to say goodbye.